# Teaching NLP in the Classroom

**Also available in the Ideas in Action series**

*Behaviour Management* – Tony Swainston

*Creative Assemblies* – Brian Radcliffe

*Creating an Inclusive School* – Mal Leicester

*Encouraging Reading* – Susan Elkin

*Effective Learning* – Gavin Reid and Shannon Green

*Emotional Literacy* – David Spendlove

*Implementing Personalised Learning* – Reggie Byram

*Putting Assessment for Learning into Practice* – David Spendlove

*Tackling Bullying in Schools* – Daniel Guiney

**Also available from Continuum**

*100 Ideas for Managing Behaviour* – Johnnie Young

*100 Ideas for Teaching Creativity* – Stephen Bowkett

*100 Ideas for Teaching Thinking Skills* – Stephen Bowkett

# Teaching NLP in the Classroom

Kate Spohrer

**Ideas in Action**

continuum

**Continuum International Publishing Group**

The Tower Building
11 York Road
London
SE1 7NX

80 Maiden Lane, Suite 704
New York, NY 10038

www.continuumbooks.com

© Kate Spohrer 2007

**British Library Cataloguing-in-Publication Data**
A catalogue record for this book is available from the British Library.

ISBN: 9781847060402 (paperback)

**Library of Congress Cataloging-in-Publication Data**
Spohrer, Kate E.
   Teaching NLP in the classroom / Kate Spohrer.
      p. cm. — (Ideas in action)
   ISBN 978-1-84706-040-2
   1. Communication in education. 2. Effective teaching. 3. Learning, Psychology of. 4. Neurolinguistic programming--Study and teaching. I. Title. II. Series.

   LB1033.5.S66 2007
   371.102'2--dc22

                                                        2008021937

Illustrations by Martin Aston
Typeset by Ben Cracknell Studios
Printed and bound in Great Britain by MPG Books Ltd, Cornwall

# Contents

## Chapter 4 – Internalizing NLP

## Further reading

*To my mum who I lost while writing this, my mentor, friend and greatest influence and inspiration.*

# Foreword

Thanks to Jen for reading and rereading this manuscript, without her help I don't think it would have been finished.

Throughout my teaching career, both in the classroom and as a teacher advisor, I have always believed in the premise, 'the only person whose behaviour you really have any influence over is yourself'. Accept this, act on it and 90 per cent of your battles are won. Consequently, this book might at first appear not to be what it says it is. The ideas and actions relate to the classroom but are sometimes a step away because reflection and self-change is needed before you can effect change in the classroom. Before you go further with this book I need to warn you that you are going to be asked to work a lot on yourself. NLP is a communication system and for that reason it is not something that can 'bolt on' or that can be worksheet based. For NLP to work in your classroom it needs to become part of your muscle; then you can get it into the children's muscles and that way it starts to work in the school. Read on and prepare for transformation . . .

# Introduction

It's a funny thing but I really can't remember how I first became aware of NLP. All I do know is that I became enchanted by its mystery some years ago. First I bought a book called *Brief NLP Therapy* by Ian McDermott and Wendy Jago. The book was an excellent introduction to NLP, but I realized that to really get to know what NLP is you need to really feel it in your bones. As a consequence of this, I eventually attended an NLP Practitioner course and then an NLP Master Practitioner course. The training I did was not especially geared to the field of education, but for me that didn't matter because NLP is applicable everywhere and once you enter into its world you can apply it everywhere. I could see, from the perspective of an educationalist, that what we know of as accelerated learning in education seemed to originate in the NLP stable. Many other concepts – learning styles, multiple intelligences, Brain Gym – also have a neurological aspect that links them with NLP. However, NLP is so much more than that.

Over several years working as a behaviour advisory teacher and educational researcher, casual observation has indicated to me that the basis of good teaching is a good relationship with your students. My professional quest has been to find ways to enable teachers and teaching assistants to gain this skill quickly, and nothing I have found has come up with these skills with the speed and effectiveness of NLP.

NLP was founded by John Grinder and Richard Bandler, who in the 1970s in California studied the communication styles of very gifted communicators and modelled their behaviour; they found amazing and interesting results. By modelling the way excellent communicators work, anyone can improve their communication skills, and who wouldn't want to improve their communication skills?

John and Richard wrote the seminal NLP text *The Structure of Magic 1 – A Book about Language and Therapy*. *The Structure of Magic* is a complicated read which drips with linguistic gems. Fortunately, many people have read the book and there are lots of training courses out there to help a practitioner get it in the muscle and feel it in the bones, but essentially it all stems from the creative spark of John Grinder and Richard Bandler who were able to look at excellent communicators and codify their methods.

Learn to tune into the way people process information and which senses seem to be dominant by observing their preferred communication style and mirroring that style; before long you are on their 'wavelength' and then able to build a good relationship. Once you have that you are equipped to enable your students to go further in areas they, and possibly you, never thought possible. Good education is dependant upon the relationships built up in the classroom. Think back to the teachers you remember as your favourites and who inspired you to learn. Chances are they were the ones who were excellent communicators and who you believed understood and liked you. I remember a teacher who I still hold in great esteem and was a great inspiration to me both at school and after I had left. He always started his lessons with some kind of meandering story. I used to wonder just what the point of the lesson was, but I realize now that he was actually using story or, more accurately, metaphor, to embed learning. He was preparing our unconscious minds for learning and using subliminal messages to drive home scientific points. He probably didn't realize he was doing it, he was just a naturally gifted communicator.

So what was it about NLP that seemed to draw me in so that I had to learn more? I was very sceptical for a long time; in fact, I had looked at NLP for about ten years before I went to train properly. I realize now that this was something of a waste of time – I should have gone much, much sooner, because it really works. NLP is like 'the knowledge', sounds weird I know but it's hard to describe in any other way – it's as if you have discovered something like magic. It gives you so much power and enables you to cast away limiting beliefs and use your new beliefs to do whatever you need to do.

NLP is very effective in enabling people to overcome fears, anxieties and limitations, thus allowing them to achieve more and, in the school situation, learn more effectively in life in general and become a more fulfilled and wholesome individual. This is particularly useful for children with special educational needs or behavioural difficulties. Fears and anxieties produce a lack of confidence, poor confidence leads to poor self-esteem, leading to poor learning. You need to be confident to take risks with your learning to feel the stretch and grow as a result.

So, how do we do this? Essentially, an NLP Practitioner will establish rapport very quickly with a person by carefully observing the eyes, lips, skin tone, breathing rate, activity level, actions, posture, voice timbre, tone and volume and use of language. For example, if they prefer phrases like, 'I hear what you are saying' or, 'I see what you mean', they will mirror those in the language they use, they will respect the other person's 'map of the world'. All of this helps to build up a picture of how the unconscious mind is working and then you can get into rapport with that person and make them feel comfortable and ready to learn. It's so simple – it's just what all the truly great communicators have done through the ages – Jesus Christ, Ghandi, Bill Clinton, etc. People famous for this now are the likes of Paul McKenna and Derren Brown. It is a human thing that anyone can learn – it just takes practice and feedback.

# 1 Tuning in to the NLP frequency

## Start your journal

Before you can help anyone else you need to spend a little time asking yourself a few questions. To be a good teacher, teaching assistant, parent, etc., it is helpful to know yourself quite well. You may need to be quite candid with yourself and sometimes change the way you think about and do things. This is what I call reflective practice and one of the best ways to be reflective is to keep some kind of log of your day to day professional – and private – thoughts and actions. I don't do this as well as I should but I have a friend who tells me now and again of what she wrote this time last year. She has one of those five-year diaries I think – I've never seen it – but it is fascinating to hear her reflections on what she did this time last year. You can learn a lot from this kind of journal.

Advice

The first action that I want to introduce to you is – keep a journal. You may already have a diary and that is a start, even if it only has where you are going in it, as it still gives an idea of what is going on in your life – but it can be so much more than that and so much more useful to you. This book is about getting NLP into the classroom, so in this journal think about addressing these questions first:

- How do I feel about my work in the classroom right now?
- Are there any areas or aspects of what goes on in my classroom that I would like to change?
- What have I done so far to address that change?
- How did I do that?

This last question is very important because we need to look at how we do things, and I mean exactly how, like the shapes we make, the postures we strike, to be able to move into doing something else.

- Do I know any other teachers/TAs that do things differently in a way I might like to emulate?

Once we have decided how we want to be and looked at, and examined, how people are who actually achieve the results we want to achieve, we too can model the way they do things and, lo and behold, we are very likely to come up with similar results.

# Goal setting

How good are you at setting goals?

Can you expect your pupils to set and achieve their goals when they see the adults around them not staying focused and not achieving their goals?

Some time ago I took the NLP Master Practitioner training course. The last thing we did before the end of the course was a board break. Now for anyone who is wondering what that is, it basically means you hit a piece of wood hard so that you smash it. This might sound a bit violent but in actual fact it is an extremely empowering thing to do. But there is more to it than just smashing a board. Before you break the board, time is spent thinking about where you want to be, what you want to focus on for the future – in other words, your goals. At the time, I was still working in a local authority job and feeling I wanted to do my own thing. This had been a desire of mine since I was at school, but somehow I had never quite worked out what it was I wanted to do. First it was one idea, then another and none of them were followed for long enough to get me out of working for someone else and really getting the buzz of working for myself. On my board I wrote 'focus' because I knew that all the great ideas in the world come to nothing in practice if you can't focus. I smashed my hand through that board and a few months later I had left my job and was going solo with a new and clear focus.

I still have the board.

Try discussing these ideas with your class and remember, at all times model good goal setting and sticking to goals if you want younger people to follow you:

- When we decide to do something we stick with it.
- I keep focused on the things I will get by reaching goals.
- These benefits are what help me keep going and drive me towards my goals.
- We set goals we know we can get and we achieve them.

# Building rapport through matching language

A fantastic place to start on building a good relationship quickly is to attain good rapport with the other person. Basic NLP provides a toolbox of techniques that offer ways of doing this effortlessly and unconsciously. Of course, it does take a bit of time to learn but with a little practice anyone can become a better communicator and build better rapport with those you wish to. It's amazing the way a little investment in learning these things can pay dividends in the classroom, in relationships, in life. Everyone benefits.

Imagine being able to understand unconscious communication, and how to communicate with the unconscious by using language patterns that make your powers of persuasion hard to resist. Listening to the language people use gives you clues as to how your pupils process language. If you can mirror their style more accurately, you can enhance your communication with your pupils, allowing you to harmonize with them and draw out the learning more effectively. If that is something you would like to know more about, have a go at the exercise below.

Advice

As you are talking to pupils try to become more and more aware of which of their senses they seem to be experiencing the world through. Phrases like 'Oh, I see what you mean!' or 'Oh, I understand now!', or 'Oh, I hear what you are saying', 'I feel can do it now', all give clues as to how an individual operates. What you need to do to increase your rapport is to match their language. If you have been talking to someone in the wrong modality you might as well have been talking in a foreign language because they just won't be resonating with you. If someone gives you a clue by saying, 'I get the picture', you continue the conversation using visual language. It's easy – try it, you'll be surprised how much more meaningful conversations will become, and how quickly you will feel the unconscious shift into rapport, when you feel suddenly you are swimming alongside someone going in the same direction in harmony, rather than swimming against the tide and feeling you will soon drown.

Application

# Gaining rapport through matching the voice

Gaining rapport is the key to excellent communication. We can gain rapport in a number of ways and, ideally, we use a number of ideas all together to establish quick and easy rapport. You can practise different aspects of rapport skills which, when put together, will blend synergistically and produce great results. One way is to concentrate on the rate of breathing and the vocal quality of the speaker. Have you ever noticed how, if you listen to someone with a different regional accent to yours, you begin to find yourself slightly taking on some of the intonation of that person? You may even pick up phrases and nuances of their speech. This is because you are falling into rapport with them; you have an unconscious desire to communicate more effectively with them and so you make yourself more like them to enable you to do that better. It isn't mimicking or taking the mickey, it is flattery and a normal response to another human being you want to communicate with. Imagine then that you don't particularly warm to someone, but you know that for work purposes you need to get on well with this person.

Advice

Focus on the child in the class who you find hardest to get on with. Observe the timbre of their voice, is it high or low, does it range a lot or a little, does it grate on you or is it mellifluous? What is the volume like, the speed of delivery?

It is very likely that however they talk it is in stark contrast to your preferred speech pattern; but you are there to communicate with your pupils and one of the presuppositions of NLP is, 'the meaning of communication is the response you get'. If you are not succeeding with a child, your communication method needs to change and maybe a slight change in your timbre to match theirs might just be enough. Play around with this idea until you feel more resonance with the child's speech.

Work on totally establishing rapport. Notice feelings of comfort and discomfort as they occur. Notice what is going on internally in your body as well as externally. Notice *feelings* as you go in to rapport. After a few minutes you should notice the physiological feelings of rapport. Also look for outward signs of rapport.

## Further action

Now you have mastered matching the voice, you can teach this amazing skill to your pupils. Get them in pairs or, better still, threes so that one can be an observer, to talk to each other and try to match the tone of each other's voices. The best way is to sit with their chairs back to back so that they are not distracted by other signs of rapport going into the other senses; this is a very auditory exercise. Mix boys with girls to make it a bit harder. Add an extension exercise to match the size of the pieces of info (length and depth).

Application

# Pacing – getting into step

In conversation with a friend of mine the other day, somehow we got to talk about walking in step. She said, 'Have you ever noticed how, when we are walking along the street, we always seem to be in step with each other, even though we have different-sized legs? That's something I don't get with everyone, some people walk so quickly I just can't keep up, they rush me, then others are so slooooow I get frustrated and impatient and then I'm the one going off ahead.'

In fact that walk is actually a metaphor for our relationship. This same principle can be applied to loads of situations, not just walking along the street with a good friend.

A young teacher, in her second year of teaching, one September described observations of her new class: 'They are so different from my last class. I know that they are a year younger but it has really brought into sharp focus the relationship I had with my old class – the great rapport we had. But you know, I think I can speed up that rapport building by gauging the natural pace of the group. It's almost like finding a kind of "resonant frequency" for the group and when I have hit on that I can harmonize with them and the result will be doubly good if I can resonate too.' I loved this description. Although it is all about sound waves, to me it created great visual appearances of waves doubling in size and energy being harnessed for everyone's benefit, a real gathering of momentum.

Advice

When we work with groups of people our task is not just to get into rapport with individuals but to get into rapport with the group as a whole. We need to sense where that group is and it will not be going at the same speed as the individuals because those speeds are all different. The group itself forms its own identity; with a little reflection you can sense that and work with it, not against it.

Over the week, keep a note of the mood of your class, with particular reference to pace. Use the table below to help prompt your observations. You may also reflect on what you found and what you did intuitively to gain better rapport. You will know when you have rapport with your class because they will effortlessly follow your lead. Remember, this is simply observing what is going on in the room and what your response is. Later, we can look at more appropriate responses that can lead your group more effectively.

|  | Observation | Response |
|---|---|---|
| How fast/slow is the settling down time? | | |
| Who is setting the pace? | | |
| What is the general completion of work time? | | |
| Did you achieve what you wanted to? | | |
| Are you trying to put too little or too much into lessons? | | |
| Where do you believe the ideal pace lies? | | |
| Any other questions relating to pace | | |

# Body and mind inextricably linked

Anything happening in the mind also happens in the body and vice versa. This has particular implications for our body language. We all give off unconscious signals that other peoples' unconscious minds pick up on. We will then elicit more unconscious communication and sometimes we wonder why someone has behaved towards us in the way they have, when in fact if we could just understand these unconscious signals we would not be half as perplexed. On a conscious level, if we act as if we are pleased to see someone our mind will respond to that and begin to be more kindly disposed to that person. Sometimes we need to get our body to go through the motions of something – to get it in the muscle – and then we actually begin to really feel those feelings inside. In the context of health, Deepak Chopra has written a lot on how the mind and emotions affect the body's healing systems (*Quantum Healing*, 1989).

Advice

Look at sensory signals. Ask another person to think of something they like a lot. You can suggest they see what they saw when they last saw this thing, smell what they smelled, feel what they felt.

While they are recalling this lovely thing, notice the expressions, skin colour, skin tone, etc.

|  | Like | Dislike |
|---|---|---|
| Eyes | | |
| Lip size | | |
| Lip shape | | |
| Head position | | |
| Breathing rate | | |
| Breathing position | | |
| Foot position | | |
| Hand position | | |
| Skin colour | | |
| Skin tone | | |
| Any twitches | | |
| Facial expressions | | |
| General comments | | |

Now, in the same way, ask them to think of something they dislike intensely. Make the same observations.

Now ask the person to choose which one they wish to think about so that we can guess which one it is. What did you notice about the unconscious signs?

# Setting goals right now for today

Goal-setting a long way into the future can be a bit daunting when you first begin and, for the students you really want to get to – who probably don't have a great sense of looking ahead – long-term goals could be a lost cause at the moment. This isn't a problem, we just need to see it from their perspective, get into pace with them and start where they are.

Today's actvity is to look simply at goals for today. Some of your students may have behaviour programmes that help them to reflect on their behaviour frequently throughout the day, but others will not have such a focus.

Advice

Take time at the beginning of the day to suggest these goals. You can do this in a number of ways – one teacher who used daily goal setting successfully had a board in the classroom and each day there was a different daily goal which greeted the students as they arrived. It's a bit like your own 'prayer for the day' or 'thought for the day' (if you are a Radio 4 listener). These regular, habitual times to refocus set up good habits, a little like an anchor – student comes into the room, looks at the board, the board has some words of inpiration, on and hey presto! – you are inspired for the day because those words will be in the unconscious mind all day and will be working away without any conscious thought. Your task is to keep the board replenished with a short collection of wise words. Here are some examples:

- Today I'm putting my best effort into everything I do.
- I enjoy my work, no matter what I'm doing.
- I see problems as learning opportunities.
- I focus on solutions and I find them.
- I am getting better at everything I do.
- I believe I can learn anything.

Of course, this is a very small and generalized selection. You will tailor your words to the mood of the group; there may be particular issues that seem especially relevant to everyone which you will want to address this way. If you can give your board a pithy and witty title all the better. I remember being in a staffroom where the head used this kind of technique on a weekly basis but the board was entitled 'Thought for the weak'. I liked that one, somehow it gave hope!

Application

# Limiting belief–busting

We all have beliefs about our ability that hold us back. I remember a story about a young lad called Jack in nursery school. He was often getting into trouble with the teachers because he used to be quite noisy and boisterous, as well as on one occasion smacking the teacher's bottom and throwing stones at another teacher's car. He was quickly gaining a reputation as a bad lad, even though he was only 4 years of age. One day he was overheard talking to a little friend about what they were going to do when they grew up. His friend, a 'better behaved' boy but nowhere near as bright, announced that he was going to become a chief of police. Jack replied, 'Oh, I won't be able to do anything like that because I'm too naughty'. This is a prime example of how we as adults inadvertently sow seeds of limiting beliefs in the minds of young people. This boy in fact was very bright and would probably have made an excellent chief of police, had he been able to steer his way through school without being branded too much of a trouble maker. We can only hope that this boy came into contact with inspirational teachers who helped him to gain more confidence in his ability, rather than to squash it.

What we can do as teachers is to help our pupils overcome their limiting beliefs by asking some choice questions. You might like to start by asking yourself some.

Advice

Think of a goal you would like to achieve at the moment and say it out loud to yourself – for me, the way I feel at the moment, it would probably be something about keeping everywhere tidy. So I would go with, 'I am a tidy person', 'I have great ability to keep a place well ordered'. Now reflect on how you feel when you say those statements out loud. You will probabaly be finding them hard to believe at this moment but that is normal because, after all, you are attached to your limiting belief – but you don't have to be, if you choose not to. If you were to look again at the situation and think about the areas that are how you want them – there may not be many, but think hard – and if it's an area that you see as a worthwhile goal you will already have been working away at it a little. Of course, it may be that keeping hold of that limiting belief serves a useful purpose. Maybe you need it at the moment? Or maybe you just think you do?

Ask yourself about your own beliefs.

Do your beliefs make any sense to you?

Where did this idea actually come from – was it you, or was it from some significant other way back in time, or is it a recent thing?

Does having this belief actually help you and protect you?

What is the benefit from holding this belief?

Is your belief not helping you picture how it would be if you no longer had it?

How would things differ if overnight your belief went away and in the morning you had a different one?

# There is a mind-body connection

The mind and the body are inextricably connected and cannot be broken apart. They are an integrated whole. The mind decides on everything we feel; we cannot feel pain unless our mind tells us we are feeling pain. Descartes looked at the working of clocks to try to understand the human being but of course we are not clocks and we do not operate as machines. We are living systems and the parts of our system exist by means of one another. A reductionist way of looking at things separating the parts from the system just takes us further and further away from what is actually happening in the system. We need to look at the system within which the parts operate. We know that our mind has a great control over our health. How many times have you been not a bit surprised by the absence of a student, knowing somehow that the cause of the absence was psychosomatic? Have you noticed how teachers often become ill in the holidays when they unconsciously feel that they can be ill?

Our mind then gives us our reality. There is no reality other than how our senses perceive the world and how our mind interprets this information. Remember we can only feel pain when our mind tells us so, we cannot feel pain when unconscious.

Advice

So, how can this knowledge be of any relevance in the classroom you might be wondering? We can programme ourselves to be positive or negative. The following affirmations can be used by you, or your students, to help you to be more positive and to overcome adversity:

I take responsibility for my moods

My attitude is in safe hands with me

I always find the lesson in each setback

I get back up and keep trying after a setback

I see every non-success as feedback not failure

When I succeed, I ask how I did it and learn from it

Whenever I have a setback, I ask how it happened and learn from it

All my goals give me the chance to succeed

Notice the last affirmation: there is inbuilt success in your goals. It is important to set achievable goals because we all need to feel we can tick things off our list and, if our goals are unachievable, we will continue to fail and never gain the confidence that we can succeed. Remember to set your own goals and not be bamboozled into accepting goals others set for you – and remember children need to set their own goals too.

# We only see what we believe is possible

Candice Pert, in the fabulous film *What the Bleep – Down the Rabbit Hole*, tells the story of Columbus's approach to the Americas, how the indigenous population looked from the shore and saw no ships. They had never seen these forms before and could not conceive of them, so they just didn't see them. They did see large waves, but no ships. They denied there were ships. We all do this a bit, we make stories fit our patterning. Our mind then creates our reality. Only by experiencing new things and widening our horizons can we believe more things are possible. NLP can help anyone do this. If we can bust limiting beliefs we can go to places we have never been before. Believing in something really strongly can fire up every cell in your body and make great transformations. This can be used for health, learning, confidence – the list is as long as you want it to be. If you think about your students, you probably want them to feel able to do anything you ask them to do. They may have limiting beliefs that stop them experiencing their full ability and reaching their full potential.

Advice

# Cornerstones NLP

## The menu is not the meal

This is an idea derived from Alford Korzybski who developed general semantics theory. His wording was 'the map is not the territory', but I feel that for children the use of menus and food is more familiar. The menu should not be confused with the meal it represents. We don't actually eat the menu, it is simply a representation of the meal – very useful as a guide to what we are about to eat, but not the real thing – it differs in many ways – it's on paper or a board for a start, it is flat and not generally edible. Of course this is just a metaphor, and the real meaning is that each one of us has our own interpretation of the reality 'out there' i.e. the environment we find ourselves in; we understand reality according to our map or menu. We need this and could not function without it, but we have to remember that maps and menus need to change over time; they need to be redrafted when we discover a new bit of 'reality' or our palate changes and we need a new menu.

## Guided relaxation to induce increased ability.

Sit with both feet flat on the floor.

Make sure your back is straight and your bottom as far back into the seat as it will comfortably go.

Rest your hands, palms facing upwards, on your thighs.

Think about your breathing.

Close your eyes.

Breathe in quietly; no one should be able to hear you breathe.

Breathe out quietly.

Breathe in . . . Breathe out . . .

Breathe in . . . tense your head now as tense and tight as you can get it, scrunch up your face . . . as you breathe out . . . relax.

Breathe in . . . tense your shoulders and back . . . as you breathe out . . . relax.

Breathe in . . . tense your arms, make fists of your hands, as tight as you can . . . as you breathe out . . . relax.

Breathe in . . . tense your chest and tummy as tight as you can . . . as you breathe out . . . relax.

Breathe in . . . tense your thighs and bottom . . . as you breathe out . . . relax.

Breathe in . . . tense your knees and calves . . . as you breathe out . . . relax.

Breathe in . . . tense your ankles and feet . . . as you breathe out . . . relax.

Now, as you breathe in, think of all the limiting thoughts you have telling you things you can't do and are not very good at. As you breathe out let all of those negative limiting thoughts go, let them fly away, or drain away, visualize yourself able to do all of the things you have been telling yourself you can't do. See yourself doing them now. That's right. Think how positive your thoughts are now . . . that's right . . . that's good.

Hold these pictures and feelings for a few breaths allowing them to sink in.

Now you are feeling positive and good about your ability, ready for tackling new challenges.

Enjoy that feeling for a few more breaths.

Slowly remember where you are . . .

Keeping your eyes closed, rub your hands together, place your warm hands over your eyes, open your eyes behind your hands, slowly spread out your fingers to let in the light.

## Read the eyes

In this world full of dangers, we all need to be as good as possible at checking out who are wolves in sheep's clothing. For a long time we have know the expression 'shifty eyes'. It is associated with someone you should not trust because it is felt that, if a person has shifty eyes, they are not telling the truth. Most of us like to make eye contact with a person and maintain a reasonable level of contact throughout a conversation and we get put off if their eyes keep darting about, or if they won't look at us at all. Maybe you would like to learn a bit more about what people's eye patterns really mean? Although what I am going to describe is not definitive, it does give you a framework for trying to understand the basic principles. As with all elements of behaviour, it is important to calibrate on the actual person you are trying to read and sometimes they actually work completely the opposite to most other people.

Try getting your class to 'read' each other's eye movements. This will equip them with a very important life skill that might even save their life one day.

Calibrate on eye pattern moveme[r] following questions. Watch whe[r] question – it may be better to d[ ] needs to read the question, ar[ ] dart to and the other needs [ ]

**Kinaesthetic**

What does it feel like to[ ]

**Auditory digital**

What is something y[ ]

**Auditory remembere[d]**

Which is louder, your landline o[r ]

**Auditory constructed**

What would it sound like if you played a CD, o[r ] were on the phone at the same time?

**Visual remembered**

What is the colour of the clothes you wore yesterday?

**Visual constructed**

What would your room look like if the walls were covered in gold fabric?

Now check your results with the chart below. The eye patterns are a generalization as to how **your** eyes would move if you are right-handed. The following picture describes the eye patterns for a right-handed person as **you look at them.** For many left-handed people, the chart is reversed, i.e. mirror image.

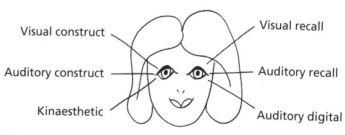

Eye Pattern Chart
Looking at the Other Person

Visual construct — Visual recall
Auditory construct — Auditory recall
Kinaesthetic — Auditory digital

Advice

Application

*Now you have been introduced to NLP and have some idea of
what it is about, it is time to look at the principles that NLP
is built on and see how that can lead to big changes in your
behaviour and, as a consequence, the behaviour of the children
in your classroom.*

Enabling children to understand different perspectives is sometimes
not easy – in fact, enabling adults to, with their more developed
sense of empathy, is often hard. The idea behind 'the map is not the
territory', or 'the menu is not the meal' is that everyone's reality is
different. One way could be to set up an art class. Take an object that
is fairly simple to draw but has something to distinguish its different
sides. A box with a bold design on might do – say, a cereal packet.
Place the object on a table in the centre of the room and arrange the
tables and chairs around in a large circle. All the children will have a
slightly different viewpoint but they all know they are drawing the
same object. Give them colours to use, oil pastels are my favourite. See
what they come up with. You can then discuss the different pictures
from different perspectives and explore the idea that, although we
may be sensing the same thing, we sense it in very different ways, so
making our own reality. You may not get as far as the philosophy with
younger children, but you could be surprised at just how far you can
get, and then you can always refer back to this class experience when
you need to help people understand that we all have our own reasons
for doing things.

Application

# Things are what we think they are

Our senses take in raw data from our environment and that raw data has absolutely no meaning whatsoever, other than the meaning we choose to give it. Alford Korzybski illustrated this in a lecture by going to his bag and explaining he needed a biscuit. He offered the biscuits around and some students took the biscuits. He then revealed the packaging more fully – dog biscuits – and the reaction from some of the students when they believed they had eaten dog biscuits was to feel sick. He said this proved people do not only eat food, they eat words too. The meaning then, that we as individuals attribute to situations, is immensely powerful. We can use that to our advantage or disadvantage. The choice is ours.

Advice

Tell the story above and use it to start a philosophical discussion of the idea. Remember when you facilitate such a discussion, it is very important to stand back and listen. Children will learn and discover more if they come up with thoughts themselves so, if you can, promote discussion by asking questions that help discussion to continue. For example, use of the phrase, 'yes, go on', when someone is stalling allows them space to keep going and dig deeper. Often as teachers we want to rush discoveries. People learn best in their own time.

# Flexibility of thought and behaviour gives more choice

In order to get different results, you need to keep doing different things. If you always do what you have always done, you'll always get what you've always got. You may have some colleagues or friends who always seem to know what to do in a difficult situation (you might be lucky enough to consider yourself to be one of these people). The chances are that they use a number of strategies and that these strategies cover quite a range. These people will be flexible in their approach, they will be unflappable, not fazed by any situation they find themselves in and probably appear quietly confident. They will be good communicators who are able to read unconscious signals and adapt to the communication styles of others and to any situation they find themselves in. Contrast this with people who are rigid and will not bend on anything. They are at a distinct disadvantage when trying to communicate well with others because their comfort range is so narrow that a lot of communication opportunities will fall outside of their range and, consequently, be lost. In your role you need to be an excellent communicator, not only with the young people you work with, but with colleagues and parents. You will need to be flexible in the way you communicate and, if you are, you will have a good picture of how things are from three different perspectives.

Advice

The next time you are faced with a challenge, model to your class different ways of thinking about how you could react. Discuss with them, take them with you on your journey through the problem-solving process. Stop and say, 'Now let's think about this', and really allow yourself to think about the problem. They will know you are delving around for solutions because they all have unconscious understanding of your eye pattern movements. Your eyes will be moving into different areas to find solutions from the past and to construct scenarios that might work in the future. If they see you coping in new ways they will find new ways to cope; after all, we want creative problem solvers don't we?

# The meaning of your communication is the response that you get

It does not matter what you meant, what matters is what actually results from your words, tone and actions. How many times have you said to someone, 'I didn't mean it like *that*'?

The fact is, though, in the other person's reality, *that* is exactly what you did mean, because *that* is the way they took it. It comes back to the difference between the map and the territory again. We have to accept that other people might not construe something the way we do so, as great communicators, we need to look again, listen to what they are saying, listen to how they are saying it, tune in, get rapport, get into their skin and communicate using their ways. That way we have a bigger chance of speaking the same language. The only person we really have any control over changing is ourselves, so if our message is not getting across and having the effect we think it should have, we need to change the way we are acting. If we try to change someone else without changing the way we respond to that person first, we will always get what we have always got from them.

Advice

This is such a useful concept in the classroom. How often we feel misunderstood; well, see it from a different perspective – you sent the wrong message. Eureka! You *can* do something about that – change the message.

# Every behaviour is useful in some context

Consider this: no behaviour is wrong in itself, it is perhaps just not the most appropriate behaviour for the context. As we go about our business as human beings we are trying to make sense of the world and do the best we can. Essentially, everyone wants to be happy, we all seek pleasure. Sometimes, though, the way we get that pleasure will be contrary to someone else and may cause significant harm. None the less, to the doer, it makes some kind of sense. It is worth appreciating that when working with challenging behaviour. Some behaviours really seem to be very contrary and go against making the life of anyone, doer or done to, any better, but look behind and you may find some kind of meaning because, to be sure, there is meaning in there. This presupposition does not give excuses or negations for bad behaviour, it just helps us to find reasons and, once we have found reasons for our behaviour, we can work towards moving away from negative behaviour patterns. Also, when we know a person's motivation, we can tune into that and appeal to their motivation to elicit good behaviour, rather than negative behaviour.

Reflect on the motive of behaviour the next time you are faced with a challenging child in the classroom. Use your rapport skills to get more in tune with the child and, gradually, using embedded commands like, 'I'm wondering?' (and others that appear in Chapter 3), see how you bring their thinking more in line with acceptable classroom behaviour.

# Praise sandwich

Lee Cantor in his books on Assertive Discipline talks a lot about praise. He recommends that teachers use a ratio of four positive comments to every negative comment in their classrooms. When this is done with sincerity it is the most magical experience you can have in a classroom. Having been an advisory teacher and spent many hours observing in classrooms, I can vouch for the tear-inducing effects of real positive teaching – yes, I have wanted to cry with joy when I have walked out of some classrooms. Michael Bernard in his system called 'You Can Do It' talks of behaviour specific feedback. Lots of children get lots of behaviour specific feedback but it reinforces the negative behaviour they are engaging in – and do you know why? Because we adults are sometimes stupid enough to keep noticing children for doing things we don't want them to do and we keep giving them attention for doing those things! It's part of human nature to seek attention and so we will all do more of whatever gets us noticed by significant others in our lives – don't underestimate the power you have over younger people.

Advice

When you need to correct a child, remember it's best done from a position of rapport, quietly and calmly. Choose a couple of things they have done or that you like about them to sandwich the negative bit you need to say to them and keep the ratio of 4:1 in your mind. If you can employ this tactic, you will be brilliant. You can also pass this amazing life skill on to your pupils by helping them to find positive things to feed back to each other when you are all engaging in class coaching sessions. Generally children are positive naturally and want to praise their peers. Don't destroy this beautiful quality, nurture it, help them to keep their cups half full, or even overflowing.

# There is no failure, only feedback

All results are useful information and can be used to propel us to success. Now you have adopted this mind shift you will be seeing how much more positive the whole world is. The other great thing about this is that you can use it so much with the young people you work with. Just by using the terminology you will be setting up more positive thinking about the self in the mind of the young person. By asking, 'what's the feedback?' and then going through this as a positive piece of information which can be built on, you can really help young people to grow in self-esteem and confidence. In addition it is a good idea to talk about feedback you have received during your week. It may be that you have had some feedback from one of your own family members, friends or colleagues which it is OK to talk about. By doing this you model that it is normal to receive feedback throughout your life and that you welcome it and use it to help you to do things differently next time if necessary. It may be that some of the young people you work with don't often see adults around them coping well with feedback.

Advice

Alter the language in the classroom – drop the use of 'failure, 'see me', 'ways to improve', in fact any term you have been using that could have a negative connotation and use the word 'feedback' for an all round appraisal of a piece of work. It is essential to use it with enthusiasm, remember once you have rapport with your class you will be able to spread enthusiasm for feedback just by being enthusiastic about it yourself because you will be leading and they will be taking their cue from you, but only if you have gained that all important rapport. Use the term with gusto, communicating that feedback is a great thing to get – well it is, isn't it? It helps you improve, so it's got to be good, don't you think? Remember though that giving feedback has to be done skilfully.

Application

# See your communication as inflexible, rather than your pupil as resistant

Something will work. If you look deep enough and try enough things, you will definitely find something that works. The word 'client' here might sound a bit off-putting but, if you can think in terms of the client being the child, it might make more sense. In our role as the adult around the child we need to keep trying to find ways to communicate effectively with the child so that the response we get from our communication is the one we want to get. If we get a different one, we need to find another way. In Greek mythology Procrustes had an iron bed onto which he invited guests to lie down. If the guest proved too tall, he would cut the legs, if the guest was too short, he was stretched out until he fit. If we want to behave like Procrustes we can expect everyone else to fit our standard. However, it would seem more sensible to try to adapt and maybe have a bed that can be more accommodating. (In fact, Procrustes used to secretly adjust the bed when he saw the size of the guest ensuring a bloody end every time. Fortunately Theseus put a stop to all of this by putting Procrustes in the bed prepared for Theseus – a short stout fellow – so Procrustes lost his head and feet.)

Take the child in the class you find most difficult to communicate with. Work hard at building rapport, make an extra special effort to do this and see how, as you build rapport, you begin to like the child more and they seem to like you more. See also how you are becoming more flexible in the way you communicate. You may even find yourself saying, 'I would never have dreamed of saying that a few weeks ago', and you might find yourself starting to extend how you interact. Notice too how your class is starting to build better rapport with each other. Everyone benefits.

Application

# The three Rs – Rapport Reduces Resistance

We will move heaven and earth for those we love and want to impress. When you have rapport, you have massive influence. Sometimes in our work we need to act as if we really love the young people we work with, even when we feel we don't. During my training my mother, a retired headteacher, used to say to me, 'You have to love your children'. She is right, if you want to get the best out of them you have to really value and cherish them. If you take time to get into rapport, to get into the way they are thinking, you will find communicating and leading them through learning so much easier. If they resist you, go back and look at *your* rapport skills. Think about what you need to do to put them at their ease, to level with them and to make them feel you accept them for what and who they are, that you are meeting them where they are, not where you want them to be. You will know when you have rapport, you can just feel it and things change. It's as if you were swimming around in the sea and suddenly, instead of swimming some distance away from each other, you start swimming alongside each other, going along together smoothly, making progress in unison. Your movement in the water creates mutually helpful currents, it becomes a symbiotic experience.

Advice

Keep building your rapport skills – aim for a symbiotic relationship with your pupils – you need them as much as they need you. If you feel you have any areas of rapport that are a bit lacking work them up – remember rapport building is best if you match:

- body movements
- size of information chunks
- volume of voice
- pitch of voice
- tone of voice
- topic interest
- breathing rate.

Look at your own behaviour in those areas. Be critical, give yourself some honest feedback, imagine looking on from a third-person perspective, be self-aware. Only by being good at building rapport yourself can you pass on this amazing skill to your class. You can do it!

# We already have all we need

All the resources we need are inherent in our own physiology and neurology. This is such an empowering idea to hold onto. Think about children and adults you know who keep making excuses as to why they can't do something. Often they will try to make you believe that circumstances beyond their control are stopping them from doing things and this is a convincing argument that you might really go along with for a long time. In fact you might even do a little bit of this yourself. Think though for a minute how it would feel to truly believe that you can affect your own success. One of the great things about NLP is that it opens your mind up to new possibilities. You cast away limiting beliefs that have been holding you back for years and years and become open to success. Each one of us has what we need to succeed.

When next a child tries to convince themselves, and you, that they cannot do something, ask them: 'What is the worst thing that could happen if you did (the thing that they think they can't do)?' 'What would you not have if you (did it)?' 'What would you have if you (did it)?'

Questions like these can help the brain imagine the thing they can't do, done!

# We create our own experience

We are responsible for what happens to us. Once we can accept that we have the resources we need, it is only one small step to move into making things happen that we want to happen. If we don't make something happen that we have decided we want and we still really want it, we need to go back, look at what we are doing and do it differently. If it isn't working, change the way we do it. Look at the way successful people operate in this field. What are they doing that you aren't? Is there something you could learn from someone else?

Advice

With your class, take a person who they consider to be successful. You can do this individually or, if you like, as a whole class. You may like to tie it in with a show like *X Factor* or *Strictly Come Dancing* – anything that shows success comes with perseverance and a belief in oneself. Look at the characters and deconstruct what makes them successful. At a future time, refer the class back to these people and how they 'do' success – encourage your class to copy the positive aspects of the behaviour.

# Putting your mouth where your money is

## Get your cup to overflow

I work a lot with children and families affected by two very different conditions: ADHD and EB. EB (Epidermolysis Bullosa) is a very rare, inherited debilitating skin disease in which the skin and internal body linings blister at the slightest knock or rub, causing painful, open wounds. ADHD (Attention Deficit Hyperactivity Disorder) is a condition affecting concentration, attention, impulsivity and activity, frequently causing problems in social and educational settings. Both of these very different conditions can cause the sufferer to think that they are EB or ADHD and that is that! It seems to be hard for people to disassociate themselves from the condition and somehow it takes over and is the reason and cause for every problem in life. This is a mental attitude and we can change our attitude to change our outcomes. We all have problems, whether we have a label or not, and sometimes it is difficult to work out why. In fact, sometimes there is no point in trying because what we really need to do is to work out what we want and are going to do. As individuals we create our world and we can take responsibility for what happens to us. As teachers and TAs, we have a wonderful world in the classroom. We can make amazing things happen in there. Someone was talking about Bill Clinton on the radio. They said that he has an incredible quality and lit up rooms when he walked in, that he was so popular as president that if the American Constitution allowed it, he would have been in for a third term. They also said Bill 'isn't a half-empty or half-full man, his cup is overflowing'. Wow!!! That is mental attitude. Are you half-full or half-empty?

*NLP is largely concerned with using language persuasively. This chapter gives many examples and exercises in using language effectively.*

In your lessons become aware of how often you use these words and phrases:

- You can do that
- Yes
- I like that
- I like the way you are . . .
- We will
- I am able to
- You are able to
- How do you do that?

You will see the theme of these phrases and words are all positive. We get positive results when we project positivity into the world. Conversely, if you wake up grumpy and stay grumpy, projecting grumpiness, guess what, you'll see lots of grumpy people that day. If you project an aura of being able to cope with everything life throws at you, your class will too. If you have ever been to see any of the 'Die Hard' films you almost certainly won't have been able to walk out of the cinema with anything but a smile on your face – it's just all so positive and makes you feel full of wonderful endorphins. You come out on a real high, ready to tackle the world. I'm not suggesting we get violent here but there is nothing wrong with borrowing a bit of enthusiasm, is there?

# Reframe

By using positive language to reframe situations, we can create a more positive world around us. We can do this for our pupils too but they will need practice and your help and encouragement to continue to grow their positivity. We also need to remember that everyone has their own interpretation of the world. Believe it or not, we all live in a different world, even though we might think that out there there is a reality. In fact there isn't because the only reality is what exists in our heads because that is what we act on and how we see things.

Advice

Try using the scenario below to help your pupils think about how they think about things.

You are playing a game in the playground and another pupil, who you don't know very well and has only ever scowled at you, knocks into you as they go past you. Do you think:

a   'They did that on purpose and meant to hurt me, I'm going to hurt them back.'

b   'They lost their balance and knocked into me by accident.'

c   'They did that deliberately to get my attention. Maybe I need to be more friendly to them. I'll smile at them and encourage them to start smiling at me.'

You will see that the three options are certainly not the only options, but representative of a range of thinking. Give the opportunity for reframing the situation and going forward with a new way of thinking that may produce a real practical change in the playground. This idea embodies both projecting what you want to receive and reframing an incident that could be viewed in a negative way. Reframing is a brilliant way to help people feel more in control of their life and thus to increase self-esteem. Once you feel you have control, you can feel so much better about yourself and experience healing. No on else can make you feel bad about yourself, you have to agree to it. This reminds me of a quotation from the Roman philosopher Marcus Aurelius: 'Take away your opinion, and then there is taken away the complaint "I have been offended". Take away the complaint, "I have been offended", and the offence is gone.'

Application

## Worst class/best class

Some years ago a teacher found herself teaching the 'worst class' in the school. She told me she didn't go into situations expecting them to be bad. This class were coming up from the feeder school and already had a formidable reputation. She did her best to take little notice of the reports and scare stories she was being fed by their current teachers. It soon became clear however that this group of young people were an interesting mix who found it hard to gel as a group and who enjoyed the sport of antagonism. Among the group were a number of overactive children and the male:female ratio was about 2:1. What was she to do? She said, 'I realized that this group of children had had lots of behaviour specific feedback, but it was negative and so they had really developed their negative side very well. My task was to reframe the whole class into a group who felt good about themselves and believed that they could do well, had some control over their actions and were the best class in the school.' How did she do it?

She used a series of affirmations with her class that gradually would be internalized in each individual's thinking and start to be played out in action. She knew she needed to spend time building rapport with them to build up a trusting relationship and to set boundaries as to what was expected and what was not. She needed to make them feel secure in her care and that she was with them not against them. In the privacy of her classroom she set about reframing the class. First, she had to truly believe that they were the best class in the school. As far as her reality went, they were. After all, they were her class. It's a bit like your own children – as good parents we believe fully in our children, that they are the best because we know unconsciously that we are there for them and have their best interests at heart. As a teacher, it is the same with your class – you have to love them. If you don't, get out of the profession.

Use affirmations on a daily basis so that you as a teacher/ TA model positive self-talk and coping strategies. Your pupils will begin to pick up on this and become more accomplished human beings.

We are the best class in the school.

Anything is possible for this class if we want to do it.

My faith in my class is strong.

I trust in my ability to get up from any and all defeats.

Application

# I'm wondering?

As teachers, TAs and parents we use suggestive language many times a day but are we aware that we are doing it? Sometimes it may be working against us because we might inadvertently be suggesting a child do something we actually don't want them to do. Psychologists tell us that the human mind cannot conceptualize the negative. If you suggest to me that I don't eat that piece of cake, the only thought I can have is about eating that damn cake! Suggest to me I have a piece of fruit and I might just eat the fruit instead of the cake. In NLP there is a concept of embedded commands. These are phrases that are dropped into sentences in conversation that might frequently not make grammatical sense and, in so doing, grab your attention, or they could be preceded by a pause or an 'uummm . . .', or a change in tone, a gesture, something that marks them out as something to be noticed, but they also suggest that you do something, that you have the confidence to do something, the power to, etc. You don't need to be in a trance to accept embedded commands but they will go straight into your unconscious mind. I had a teacher once who used to make a strange kind of flicking gesture with her hand and tilt her head a little to one side every time she introduced an embedded command. If you watch politicians and comedians you will see they are doing it too.

Advice

One of the most effective ways to embed a command is by using the term, 'I'm wondering?' Try weaving the embedded command, 'I'm wondering', into your interactions in the classroom. You can use it in so many ways, for example drop into the middle of a conversation the phrase, '. . . and I'm wondering if you can do these two questions in the next five minutes . . .', then return to whatever you were talking about before. This somewhat misplaced phrase, because of that, helps to embed the command.

# Reframing revisited

I do a lot of awareness-raising in relation to Attention Deficit Hyperactivity Disorder (ADHD). You may be aware that ADHD is deemed to be a mental health disorder; however, I don't like to think of it that way. I prefer to reframe it as a certain personality type that, for all its faults, actually has some really good aspects and an ADHD person can contribute a lot to society. One exercise I love doing on my trainings which I am going to share with you is reframing the diagnostic criteria so that we can think more positively about it.

Advice

Below are some of the diagnostic criteria for ADHD (incidentally, this condition is thought to affect 5 per cent of the school population, so over one child in every class on average). Take them and rephrase them in a positive way. You may have to be very creative here, for example take this one:

*Frequently makes careless mistakes in work, does not attend to detail.*

Could be reframed as 'willing to have a go and make mistakes', or it may also be that the pupil 'likes to get on with a task quickly and get it finished quickly'. Although we don't want to encourage slapdash work, it is sometimes great when people just go and do it!

Now try reframing these:

- Often tries to avoid tasks requiring sustained mental effort.
- Is often easily distracted by normal activity going on around him/her.
- Often fidgets with hands or feet/squirms in seat.
- Frequently out of seat.
- Usually finds he/she has to run everywhere or climb on walls/banks. In adolescence/ adulthood this may manifest itself in restlessness, e.g. leg twitching, finger tapping.
- Usually 'on the go' or acts as if 'driven by a motor'.
- Talks excessively.
- Frequently blurts out answers to questions before hearing full question.

# Using metaphor modes

In education we have heard a lot about learning styles and how we need to teach to the style of the individual student. That is all well and good, but how do you know what their style is? Sure you can do lots of paper tests and analysis, but do you really have the time for that and do you really need it? Intuitively, you have the skill to ascertain learning styles and, with a bit of fine-tuning, you will be able to switch on these skills and teach in the right style. Every one of us uses metaphor in some way. By listening to the metaphors students use, you can ascertain their predominant modality.

Metaphors create excellent pictures or sensory experiences of whatever the originator of the metaphor is feeling. Metaphor gives others clues as to how we expereince things. Sometimes, if something is outside our range of understanding and experience, the use of metaphor brings it within. James Lawley and Penny Tompkins (2000) suggest we ask a student some simple questions:

'And when you're learning, that learning's like what?'

Whatever answer comes, encourage further development with:

'And is there anything else about that X?'

(X being the metaphorical part of the answer to the first question)

'And what kind of X is that X?'

So, in practice you find that people have a wide range of metaphors and they may be very different from the ones you would use yourself – which is where your task as a teacher really comes into play. You need to be aware of your own style and make sure you use a wide enough range of metaphors to appeal to others who may be of different style to you.

If you ask a pupil, 'and when you're learning, that learning's like what?' They might say:

- Well, it's like wading through treacle.
- It's like soaring through the air.
- It's like eating something really hard to chew and swallow.
- It's like giving birth.
- Learning for me is like painting a picture.
- Learning is like a long, long journey and I think I will be on it, till the day I die and beyond – who knows.
- Always for me, it's like being in the dark for a while and then the light comes on and I can work it out.

You can see from the above examples that people's metaphors on the learning experience differ – in fact, they will differ according to what they are learning. Thinking about maths may give a very different metaphor to thinking about language.

Ask your students the above questions, note the responses and ask yourself, 'Am I communicating in enough metaphorical modes?'. You may want to increase your repertoire. It isn't difficult, but you do need to raise your level of consciousness (which you will have done by reading this) and you will match metaphor modes more easily. See how much less resistance to your suggestions you get in the classroom, or even at home.

# Using embedded commands to aid homework

How would you like to send your pupils away from your lesson with an embedded command to do their homework? Well now you can. Embedded commands are dropped into speech and sit in the unconscious mind ready to pop up at just the right time. As part of your closing routine or plenary for the lesson, you can settle your class and send them on their way with a great gift by using a script like the one opposite. It is best read quite slowly and deliberately and I would even start with a brief relaxation and ask for eyes to be closed. Maybe even deliver it from the back of the room provided you do not have any children with hearing impairments who may need to keep their eyes open and watch your lips. The script is inspired by the work of Milton Erikson and is often referred to as the Milton Model.

Use this script at the end of your lesson or the day to help embed commands for learning. Not only will it help students do their homework but it will embed the learning from the lessons they have had that day.

'So, as you begin to hear this, and I suppose (and it's a good thing to make such assumptions, now . . . and again) . . . because it means . . . you are learning everything you need from this lesson as all those things . . . everything, that you can learn . . . give you new skills and knowledge. And you can, can't you? – learn, that is, by listening. And it's more or less the right thing for you right now, isn't it? I mean, while you are sitting here, listening to these words consciously, it means your unconscious mind is also here and can hear these words. And, since that is true, it's not right for me to tell it – learn these things now, or later when you are doing your homework – let it learn them any way it wishes, in any order. Do you feel this . . . is it something you can understand? Because what you have heard today speaks to your unconscious mind more than your conscious mind. Whether you begin to use what you have learnt today straightaway or later when you do your homework is not so important because I know you are a conscientious student – and it's good to be a conscientious student, as conscientious students are successful. And success is everyone's goal, isn't it?'

# Affirmations empower

One really effective way of improving the way you are is to use affirmations. I have talked about affirmations earlier in the book, but, in case you missed them, here is a simple affirmation game to help you make each day a little more positive in some way or other for you and your pupils.

Copy onto card and cut up the affirmations. You may need to copy more than one set or make up some more affirmations. Each child picks an affirmation for the day and uses it for that day. Alternatively, you can ask a child to pick for the whole class and use the affirmation for the group. See which works best for you. The aim is to get children into the habit of positive self-talk.

| I'm getting started on important tasks today. | I get a lot done because I begin. |
| --- | --- |
| I enjoy starting and finishing challenging tasks. | I can do whatever I set my mind to. |
| I'm a truly creative and imaginative person. | I treat others how they want to be treated. |
| I get back up and keep trying after a setback. | A minute wasted is gone forever – I use every minute well. |
| Today I am cool, calm and collected. | I think before I act. |
| Each day I grow more able to complete my school work. | Each day I am a little more confident than yesterday. |
| I learn something valuable from everyone. | My homework today is doable. |
| I visualize positive outcomes and they happen! | Things are never as bad as we imagine. |

# What, specifically, do you mean?

The Gestalt therapist Fritz Perls was studied by Bandler and Grinder when they were codifying what we now refer to as NLP. Perls worked on helping people to understand how they interacted with others with a view to them then being able to change those interactions if they so desired, or to carry on in the same way but to understand why they got the reactions they got.

If you can get some of this language 'into the muscle', or into your 'portfolio of skills', you will be able to pull it out of your portfolio at any time and use it with anyone.

Advice

Practise recovering bits of information from children in your class when they say the following kinds of things:

| | |
|---|---|
| He annoys me. | How, specifically, does he annoy you? |
| They all hate me. | Who, specifically, hates you? |
| No one cares about me. | No one? |
| She is better than me. | Better at what, specifically? |

Always remember to ensure rapport, make your tone match theirs and gradually bring them down to a softer, more receptive tone. Keep any accusative tone or impatience out of your voice – act as if you are the most patient person you know, visualize them and be that person.

# Challenge generalizations – 'Always?'

Sometimes in speech we make sweeping generalizations. These follow through from our speech to our thinking and can manifest themselves as limiting beliefs. A limiting belief has the effect of stopping us from achieving our potential and no one really likes that, do they?

## Challenge generalizations when you find them.

This is very easy to do, for example when a child says something like, 'I always get told off in that lesson', you can answer, 'Always?' Remember you need to say the word always with a questioning intonation, but without judgement – you may need to practise this. Convey that you are happy to accept your student's judgement and viewpoint, but maybe after a little bit of reflection you can tease out just what 'always' means in this context. It could be anything from a couple of times in the last six months to 80 or 90 per cent of the time. I recall when working as a behaviour advisory teacher that other teachers would tell me about children they were having problems with who 'never' behaved well in the classroom and 'always' played up. Well, I wish I'd done my NLP training years earlier because I know I would have been able to be a lot more useful if I had just used this little linguistic device. It's a good thing to reflect on what we really mean when we use generalizations. Helping children to look at the times they don't get told off or, in the teacher's case, when the child doesn't misbehave, can give us a much more accurate, balanced and positive perspective from which to work. Try this at home too. The next time you have a bit of a spat with your partner and have the thought, 'S/he always does that when I do this . . .' check out with yourself if always is really what you always mean!

# Generalizations 'never'

How often do we say something 'never' happens when in actual fact it does? I sometimes travel by train and am pleasantly surprised by the number of times the trains run on time – I am in fact on a train as I write this and this train was on time. Think though how negative people can become when a train is late once, how easy it is to get into the habit of saying 'these trains "never" run on time'. What this does is set up negative feelings within ourselves, it stops us enjoying each moment because we are miserable about a train that is going to be late (even when the chances are it will be on time).

Advice

Challenge 'never' and feel better chemicals enter your bloodstream. In just the same way you can challenge any generalization (like for example 'always') when it is used for negative purposes, so you can challenge 'never'. Just repeating the work in a questioning intonation is often enough to promote the speaker to question their thinking. It may take a few goes to get your class trained in this one but very soon you will notice you say, 'Never?' and they will reflect and analyse and, even better, they will drop using never and begin to move to a more positive mindset. Now, that must be something you want for your class, isn't it?

# I couldn't possibly

Whenever we hear someone say 'I can't' or more elaborately, 'I couldn't possibly do that', we know we are facing a limiting belief. In NLP we believe we have all the resources we need to do whatever we need to do, so if we say we can't do something we are stopping ourselves from doing something. If we really want to do something we can but we scare ourselves with reasons why not. We can, on the other hand, move heaven and earth when we believe we can do something – it is all in the mind. Often we are scared of the unknown, so it's a good idea to play around in the imagination, thinking about what it could be like if you cast aside fears and did do what you need to do.

Advice

The next time you say, 'I can't', or one of your pupils says this to you, say, 'What stops you? What would happen if you did? Try it? Stay with the exploration of what it would be like, visualize the situation, for a while allow it to sink in. Imagine how life would be different if you did . . .'

# Have you really got to . . . ?

While we are fretting about what we have got to do we can be missing out on what is really important. Some years ago a friend pointed out to me there is a difference between what is urgent and what is important. The urgent stuff, if it doesn't get done, often ends up not so urgent. The trick is to be able to distinguish what is important and do that. Often the stuff we think we have got to do, we haven't.

Advice

Ask yourself how many things you feel you have to do in your classroom, then ask 'What would happen if I didn't do that?'. I remember a time when I went to see a teacher who was getting her class to sit on the carpet during the early days of the Literacy Hour (as it was then called). You may recall that there were directives about what to do at various points during the hour and one of these was to have children sat on the floor. Sometimes, though, this didn't suit a class, or particular children – they fidgeted, bumwalked and generally didn't do much literacy. This was happening in this classroom. I had been called in as an advisory teacher for behaviour. I asked the class teacher why she was sitting her class on the floor and the only answer was that was what the literacy hour said she must do. Must? I asked her what would happen if she didn't do this and she was hard-pressed to find any negatives. Sometimes we really don't know why we are doing things. When you know why, you can justify your actions. That gives you confidence; all you need to do is reflect a little. Get your pupils to do it too and their critical thinking skills will multiply.

# Can you mind read?

We unconsciously assume we know what someone else is thinking. Children do this a lot because they operate at an egocentric level for at least the first decade of life, sometimes finding it difficult to discriminate between their own thoughts and someone else's, adding their own fantasy of meaning to another's actions that could be totally wrong. As adults we can also be caught doing this.

Advice

The next time a child complains to you that someone doesn't like them because they, e.g., 'stick their tongue out at me', ask, 'How do you know?', 'How does it mean she doesn't like you?' In provoking reflection, you can steer the child towards a less egocentric way of looking at the world. Introduce the idea that there are other ways of interpreting things and, by asking 'How?' as opposed to the usual 'Why?', we can explore the behaviour that is 'telling' us what someone else is thinking. When you start to do this you see things in another way and sometimes the teacher can learn from the pupil.

Application

# Who says?

When you hear the words:

'It's not right to do . . .'

'It's not right to be . . .'

'It's not right to say . . .'

'It's not right to expect . . .'

does anything occur to you? Do you get a little voice popping into your head saying, 'Who says?' If so, well done because that is exactly the kind of question we should be asking. Too often human beings behave like lemmings, just following what they have been told without question. Sometimes it's good to challenge and ask 'Who says?'

The next time you hear 'It's not right to . . .' pose some of these questions back:

'Who says it's not right?'

'How do you know it's not right?'

'What evidence do you have to support that claim?'

It may be that there is a very good reason for not doing, being, saying or expecting . . . or whatever, but it's a good thing to check it out. After all, we all like to make sure we are acting for the right reasons with the right motives, don't we?

# Switch on happiness, switch off anger

Sometimes we attribute the cause of how we feel to someone or something external to ourselves. Some psychologists would call this having an external locus of control. People with an internal locus of control feel far more able to affect their own destiny than those with an external one. An internal locus of control means we feel buffeted from pillar to post reacting to what the world throws at us and just about coping, or worse if we are unlucky. An internal locus enables us to keep our hand on the tiller and ride the rough seas. It also enables us to set out our own goals and pursue them. Our language can give away where our locus of control lies. If we confess that so-and-so 'makes me so angry', we are showing that, at that point at least, we have a tendency towards an external locus of control. Sure, it's good to be in touch with your emotions and feelings, but it is also good to be able to channel them for positive rather than destructive purposes.

Advice

One way to start is to tease out how someone makes you angry, happy, sad or whatever. If you ask, 'How specifically does he make me angry?' 'How specifically does he make me happy?', you can begin to work out what it is that causes the effect. Then, when you know the cause, you can work towards changing situations or, better still, changing the way you look at situations that you feel are making you experience negative feelings, stopping yourself getting into more situations or thinking more thoughts that make you happy. You can switch on happiness and switch off anger.

# You can interpret more accurately

Sometimes we draw conclusions based on very shaky evidence. In fact, we seem to link things together that, when looked at rationally and logically, have no link other than the supposed one in our mind. If we work out the stages we have gone through to come to the conclusion, sometimes we can see the error of our judgement. In the meta-model this is called 'false equivalences'. For example, you may judge a parent to be 'a bad parent – they encourage their children to use foul language'. Does this one piece of information provide enough evidence to make such a judgement? If we look at the reasons behind why they encourage foul language we may learn something. Maybe they are engaging in progressive parenting where they demystify early on the use of foul language. We could draw the conclusion they are misguided but not necessarily 'bad'. However, this is really playing with semantics.

Can you use this idea in the classroom? Can you challenge your pupils when they make false equivalences? For example, if a child said to you of another teacher, 'She is a bad teacher, she is always shouting at people', could you challenge this judgement by asking, 'How does her shouting mean she is not a good teacher?' I have known teachers who shout who were also good at teaching but shouting is not normally something I would recommend. However, shouting alone doesn't make everything you do unworthy. As a teacher too we can apply this to our own thinking. Are we drawing conclusions from very shaky evidence?

## Be specific!

Sometimes we talk about others in very unspecific, fuzzy ways. We might say, 'I like her', but we are not clear about what it is we like about her. The use of the word 'nice' always used to be discouraged because it really doesn't mean very much but there are lots of words like this that leave so much unsaid and misunderstood. How many times have you heard a teenager say, 'He is so annoying!!' What does he or she mean by this? How specifically is he so annoying?

Listen out for unspecified verbs, ask for clarification, find out exactly what behaviour it is that is so annoying, then you can start to work out how that situation can be avoided in future. Also ask if there is anything that the complainant does that could be precipitating the annoying behaviour. Remember, what we give out we will get back. If we want to be treated well, we have to get into rapport with the other person and lead them in the direction we want them to go. Hard work for many teenagers but not impossible. Teach your students these skills whatever age they are and they will become much better communicators and be forever in your debt.

# Using sleight of mouth patterns

Sleight of mouth was devised by Robert Dilts, who examined language patterns of excellent communicators like Ghandi, Socrates and Bandler. Sleight of mouth statements are used to challenge the unhelpful and negative belief of another. The desired outcome is a change in that belief. You can see that this device is likely to be very helpful in the classroom where a child believes they are incapable of doing something, whether it be academic or behavioural.

Take, for example, the common assertion of some children, 'I can't draw'. You can challenge this belief by asking questions that reframe:

'Yes, you don't seem in the right mood to draw at the moment.'

'Is this your way of saying you want to do something else?'

'How do you know you can't draw?'

'Do you remember the drawing you did yesterday for . . . which was very good?'

'Can you remember when you told me you couldn't do . . . and how good you are at that now?'

'You seem to find it very easy to say you can't do something.'

'What exactly do you mean by "can't draw"?'

'It's just your perception that you can't draw.'

'Who are you comparing yourself with?'

'By the end of the topic you won't even be able to remember you thought you couldn't draw.'

'You feel right now that you can't draw.'

You can see from all of these statements and questions that none are confrontational – all encourage the listener to reframe their views.

Use sleight of mouth to reframe.

You can use the style of statements below and apply to any situation where you are faced with limiting negative statements in the classroom, for example:

'When you say you can't draw, it tells me that you feel you need to learn more about drawing techniques. When you feel you need to learn more, it means that you are approaching your learning intelligently and maturely, doesn't it? And you know that when you approach things in a mature way, you will work through problems and challenges and succeed in conquering them, so saying you can't draw isn't a bad thing because it means you are assessing what you need and that helps you to find ways to get what you need and achieve your goals.'

So, using this technique, you can show that you are listening to the child who says they can't draw and not just brushing their view under the carpet.

# 4 Internalizing NLP

## Get into the alpha state to learn

When I was training to be a teacher, I remember one of our tutors advising us to watch good teachers and model what they did. From a very early age we watch what other people do and we start to copy their actions. Initially, we don't think consciously about what we are doing. As babies our unconscious mind will be taking us through these actions. Gradually we work out what effect things have and we build on the learning. Have you ever noticed how sometimes, when we are trying to learn how to do something, we actually get worse at it as we start to think too hard about it? In NLP we need to get into the 'know nothing state', or the 'alpha state' before we start to model another person. This means as far as possible we empty our mind, a bit like meditation, and then copy the skill we want to achieve.

Advice

*This chapter helps you to internalize NLP by physical practice. Remember, the more you practise NLP the more it will become embedded in your unconscious mind and show itself in your actions without you having to think about it.*

Try using music with your class to get them into the alpha state and ready for learning. You will, no doubt, have heard the term 'the Mozart Effect' which claims some of Mozart's music is particularly good at enhancing learning because it induces the alpha state. Try also some slightly more contemporary music like Mike Oldfield's 'Tubular Bells'. You can condition your class to coming into the classroom and hearing certain types of music that prepare them for learning. Try it and see what a difference it makes.

# Further learning through trance states

Some years ago, I was involved in a school project where we started the day with a few minutes of quiet reflection. The idea was to improve behaviour levels in the school by spending about three minutes at the beginning of morning and afternoon session, with the main emphasis on breathing. Focus on breathing has, for centuries, been used as a technique to calm and quieten, and it has the effect of taking you into a trance-like state where you are more able to focus on learning. Have you ever noticed how quickly your state can change when you focus on something repetitive? Some people find driving, especially driving at night on long straight roads like the motorway, a very soporific experience. The reason is that they are being sent into a mild trance, they are hypnotized by the sounds of the engine, sounds of the tyres on the road, the motion of the vehicle, the vision of a long road ahead or it could even be the passing of one after another lamp posts. When in that kind of state, we can take in information on a different level, we are more suggestive. I am not suggesting that you hypnotize your class! But I am suggesting that you prepare them to learn by helping them to achieve a receptive state for learning. The short guided imagery below should help you to calm your class down after lunchtime.

## The 3 Gs relaxation – Glowing, Golden and Good

Sitting with both feet flat on the floor, make sure your back is straight and your bottom is as far back into the seat as it will comfortably go. Rest your hands, palms facing upwards, on your thighs.

Thinking about your breathing, close your eyes.

Breathe in quietly; no one should be able to hear you.

Breathe out quietly.

Breathe in . . .

Breathe out . . .

Imagine your body to be full of dark blue ink. That ink is all the negative things that have happened to you recently, all the arguments and cross words you have had, all the nasty things people have said to you . . . or you have said to them.

As you breathe gently imagine that the blue ink is being pushed down your body and changing into golden sunlight. Right from the top of your head, down, down, down past your shoulders, down past your arms and chest . . . your tummy and thighs . . . down past your legs and ankles . . . and down past your feet . . .

Now you have drained all of the blue ink of bad feelings down to your toes and out into a big puddle next to you on the ground.

Close by there is a drain, the ink trickles away and disappears down the drain . . . away . . . leaving you feeling glowing, golden and good . . . ready for learning this afternoon.

Enjoy that feeling for a few more breaths.

Slowly remember where you are . . . (in school, classroom).

Keeping your eyes closed, rub your hands together, place your warm hands over your eyes, open your eyes behind your hands, slowly spread out your fingers to let in the light. You are now ready for learning.

Application

# States of rapport

Have you ever noticed how difficult it is to learn something new when you are tense? You keep thinking about how hard it is and how you will never get the hang of it and the more the instructor tries to help you, the more tense you become and the worse it gets. It is like that for a lot of children a lot of the time. To learn, we need to be in a receptive state. Any hypnotist will tell you that if a person is in a trance, they will take on board ideas that their unconscious mind agrees with but that they may have been finding difficult to let in to their thinking. Teaching is all about enabling people to grow, develop, extend and, in so doing, they need to take on new ideas and patterns of thinking and behaviour. To begin to get another person into a learning state you need to gain rapport with them. Some people are so good at this you feel yourself relaxing as soon as you are in their company. But have you noticed how other people make you feel immediately tense and nervous? What's the difference and, more importantly, which one do you want to be like?

Say you want to be like the one who gets people relaxed and in a learning state quickly, quite an essential for anyone who works in education, you will be hoping to build up excellent rapport rapidly. Building rapport is easy, even with people who make you feel tense and nervous, if you follow a few simple rules.

Try this exercise with your class. A PE lesson would be a good place to start, by following the movements of another person as if in a mirror. You can then move it into the classroom to practise using with a conversation.

Use a pair of good talkers to illustrate this to the class before they try to follow. You can use the whole class as group 'coaches' who can help by feeding back to the pair who are demonstrating, under your careful guidance. In pairs, A begins to tell B about something they did last night/over the weekend, etc. B matches and mirrors A's movements. These don't have to be mirror image matching, but they do need to be pretty close to the movement the person is making in action and in time, although not necessarily simultaneous. Try to encourage conversations that go two ways rather than just one way. In addition to matching movements, you can encourage children to match sentence/phrase sizes.

What should happen is that the one who starts the conversation – A – will be drawn into rapport with B. B will then be able to steer the conversation round to putting their point of view and it is likely that A will follow, or at least begin to respond positively to B's ideas. This is what happens in any normal, positive and rewarding conversational exchange. All we are doing here is deconstructing the process so that when we are faced with someone hard to communicate with, we can consciously soften them up a little by getting onto their wavelength and making them feel more relaxed. Try this yourself and notice how hostility evaporates.

Application

# Using anchors

In NLP there is such a thing as an 'anchor'. This is a trigger for entering a different state. You will, no doubt, in the past have noticed how certain situations, actions of people, music you hear among other things, can throw you into a completely different mood in an instant. Music can be particularly poignant, as can be fragrances. The habits that we live by often act to put us into a certain kind of readiness for some further activity. For example small children often go off to sleep better if they have had a bath at night. This done regularly becomes a trigger for going to bed calmly. Routines are so important to children, and adults. In the classroom you can use this idea of setting up a trigger or anchor for learning. It will become an unconscious signal that everyone is now going to settle down to work, do a test, and be creative. You can set these things up for anything you want. The idea was most famously explored by Pavlov, who rang a bell then fed his dogs. In time the dogs salivated at the sound of the bell, regardless of the presence of food. It is worth remembering that we humans are animals and can be conditioned just like dogs can. When you smell filter coffee, if you are a coffee lover, you become drawn to having a coffee; if you aren't vegetarian bacon cooking seems to have the same 'must have' effect on most people. So how can this be translated to the classroom?

A regular activity is probably the best and easiest way to start. You know your class, don't you? You can tell when they as a group are in a state of excitement and in a flat unmotivated state. The trick is to move them through states and to the most appropriate state for the activity you have in mind for them at the time. You will need to turn up your powers of sensory acuity for this. Tune into triggers and use those triggers actively to elicit learning states. A relaxation routine could be one method, or playing music to them as they enter the room could be another.

Application

# Modelling excellence

Is there a skill that you would like your class to be really good at, or are there skills within the class that you would like to be shared around more evenly? If so, why not try getting your children to model excellence? When I went on my NLP Masters Practitioner training, we all had to get into what is called in NLP terms the 'know nothing state'. This means you get into a kind of learning-ready trance. To do this we had to throw very light, tennis ball-sized plastic balls to each other with both hands and catch with both hands. This was quite a tricky thing to do, but it does get you working in a kind of automatic unconscious way and, when you are in this state, you are more receptive to learning.

Try this with your class. Remember, though, that you need to really get well into this state, not just touch on it. Once in the required state, you can introduce something to model, so if someone is good at juggling, the rest of the class could model juggling with bean bags of koosh balls. It is all about doing exactly what the expert does without trying to analyse and change it. Really try to make the shapes of the master and you can look like a master too.

## Power spots

As teachers, we often take children into the hall or gym and ask them to find a space of their own to do some kind of PE exercise. You can also do this to put children into an empowering position. If positive states are recalled once in the space, the child can recreate the positive feelings in their physiology and then actually be in a more positive mood and do more positive actions. You don't have to be in the hall to do it, this can just as easily be carried out in the classroom. If this is something you would like to hear more about read on . . .

Advice

Have the children stand up and imagine a circle on the floor just a little way in front of them (circles are good shapes for this because they are in themselves very emotionally containing and soothing spaces). Ask them to imagine it in any way they like. Suggest it be bright, as we need this image to be uplifting and joyful. Ask them to ask themselves what colour it is? What does it look like? When you can see that they are in the desired state (and this will be evident from their faces, which will look calm, happy, relaxed and, as you have spent time with your class before, you will have unconsciously calibrated their behaviour and know when they are at ease) you can suggest they remember a time when they were very, very motivated and really, really wanted to do something, and knew that they could do it, then suggest they move into their special space. When they start to drop down from this highly elated state, suggest they step back from the space.

You can use this at any time you want to motivate your class or individual children, or even yourself.

# Giving your class confidence

Have you ever wondered how you could *give* confidence to someone? Well you can – by using the NLP technique of modelling, something that in fact we start doing as babies and never really stop. But sometimes we need to practise the art more consciously.

Advice

## Doing the walk of confidence

Sometimes your pupils will lack the confidence they require to do a certain task. To encourage confidence easily, you can get them to think of a time they were confident. If this is too hard, try getting them to think of a favourite character from the TV. When they have identified the character or the time they themselves were confident, encourage them to become really aware of all of the sensory feeling they were having at that time. Use phrases like: 'Feel what you felt, hear what you heard, smell what you smelt, see what you saw' and check that they are really there. You will know they are there because they will physically change, starting to smile maybe, or show in their own way that they are relaxing into the role of 'confidence'. When you are sure they are in the 'confident' state, get them to walk the full length of the classroom, up and down, growing more and more confident each time. You can use the rest of the class to act as 'coach'. They can give suggestions as to how to make their walk look just that little bit more confident. Feedback from other people is so important. We all give out unconscious messages and it is handy to have other people actually to tell us consciously how we are doing, but in a secure environment where we view all feedback positively (and not as failure). You can help build all sorts of states in this way, but confidence is the one I have found to be most useful as it opens gates to other achievement.

# Further reading

Canter, Lee and Marlene (2001), *Assertive Discipline: Positive Behaviour Management for Today's Classroom* (Canter and Associates).

Chopra, D. (1989), *Quantum Healing Exploring the Frontiers of Mind/ Body Spirit* (London: Bantam Books Ltd).

Grinder, J. and Bandler, R. (1975) *The Structure of Magic: A Book About Language and Therapy* (California, CA: Science and Behavior Books).

Lawley, J. D. and Tompkins, P. L. (2006) *Metaphors in Mind: Transformation Through Symbolic Modelling* (London: Developing Company Press).

Mahoney, T. (2003), *Words Work* (Carmarthen: Crown House Publishing).

McDermott, I. and Jago, W. (2001) *Brief NLP Therapy* (Brief Therapies series) (London: Sage).

Pert, C. B. (1997) *Molecules Of Emotion: The Science Behind Mind-Body Medicine* (New York, NY: Touchstone).

The Next Evolution (2006) *What the Bleep!? Down the Rabbit Hole* (DVD) (London. Revolver Entertainment).

www.katespohrer.org.uk

www.nlpworld.co.uk

www.nlpacademy.co.uk

www.youcandoit.com